Stay Safe!

Water Safety

Sue Barraclough

KT-493-358

BROMLEY LIBRARIES

3 0128 70097 5637

www.heinemann.co.uk/library
Visit our website to find out more information about Heinemann Library books.

To order:
☎ Phone 44 (0) 1865 888066
▤ Send a fax to 44 (0) 1865 314091
💻 Visit the Heinemann Bookshop at www.heinemann.co.uk/library to browse our catalogue and order online.

First published in Great Britain by Heinemann Library,
Halley Court, Jordan Hill, Oxford OX2 8EJ, part of Pearson
Education. Heinemann is a registered trademark of Pearson
Education Ltd.

© Pearson Education Ltd 2008
First published in paperback in 2008
The moral right of the proprietor has been asserted.

All rights reserved. No part of this publication may be reproduced,
stored in a retrieval system, or transmitted in any form or by
any means, electronic, mechanical, photocopying, recording,
or otherwise, without either the prior written permission of the
publishers or a licence permitting restricted copying in the United
Kingdom issued by the Copyright Licensing Agency Ltd, 90
Tottenham Court Road, London W1T 4LP (www.cla.co.uk).

Editorial: Diyan Leake and Cassie Mayer
Design: Joanna Hinton-Malivoire
Illustration: Paula Knight
Picture research: Erica Martin
Production: Duncan Gilbert

Origination by Chroma Graphics (Overseas) Ltd
Printed and bound in China by South China
Printing Co. Ltd

ISBN 978 0 431 18434 0 (hardback)
12 11 10 09 08
10 9 8 7 6 5 4 3 2 1

ISBN 978 0 431 18441 8 (paperback)
12 11 10 09 08
10 9 8 7 6 5 4 3 2 1

British Library Cataloguing in Publication Data
Barraclough, Sue
   Water safety. - (Stay safe!)
   1. Drowning - Prevention - Juvenile literature 2. Aquatic
   sports - Safety measures - Juvenile literature 3. Safety
   education - Juvenile literature
   I. Title
   363.1'23

Acknowledgements
The publishers would like to thank Robin Wilcox for assistance in
the preparation of this book.

Every effort has been made to contact copyright holders of any
material reproduced in this book. Any omissions will be rectified in
subsequent printings if notice is given to the publishers.

Contents

Swimming and playing in water
is fun.

Do you know how to stay safe
in the water?

Never go swimming on your own.

Always make sure a grown-up is watching you.

Never jump and play near water.

Always swim or paddle in a
safe place.

Never swim or paddle in deep or fast-moving water.

Always choose a beach with
a life-guard.

Never forget water can be dangerous.

Always use floats if you need them.
Always learn to swim.

Never swim straight after a meal.

Always get out of the water if you are cold or tired.

Never run or play beside water.

Always be sure there is a
grown-up nearby.

Never get into a boat without
a life-jacket.

Always take care in a boat.
Small boats can tip over.

Always remember these safety rules.

Always take care in or near the water
and you will stay safe.

Water safety rules

- Make sure a grown-up is watching you when you go swimming.
- Check the water before getting in.
- Swim or paddle in a safe place.
- Use floats if you need them.
- Learn to swim.
- Get out of the water if you are cold or tired.
- Be sure there is an adult nearby.
- Take care in boats.

Picture glossary

 float something that keeps you from going under the water

 life-guard someone who works at a swimming pool or on a beach to help people who are in danger

 life-jacket jacket that helps keep you from going under the water

Index

Notes for parents and teachers

Before reading

Ask the children why can it be dangerous near water. Talk about being safe near or in water. Ask the children if they have been to the seaside. What rules did their parents have to keep them safe?

After reading

Moving in water. Put on some suitable music and demonstrate to the children how to move in different ways, such as for paddling (on tiptoe), jumping, wading (big steps), and swimming. Call out the different activities and tell the children to move as you have shown them.

Simon Says. When what "Simon says" is dangerous, the children should put both hands in the air and look sad. When it is safe, they should fold their arms and look happy. "Simon says wear a life-jacket ... go and swim in the sea after a meal ... jump in the water without checking first ... paddle in a safe place ..."

More books to read. Near Water by Ruth Thomson, the Safety First series published by Franklin Watts, *Can You Swim, Jim?* by Kaye Umansky.